Lost Words

k.s. poetry

ISBN: 9798678418722

To all those with whom I have no words left to say

"your silence said more than your words every did"
-k.s.

CONTENTS

ACKNOWLEDGMENTS

none of this would be possible without the people that left when words still needed to be said. this would not have been possible without all of the friends that stayed, without all of the people who helped me through it all, through high school. i love you.

FORWARD

Hello, I write to you from the comfort of my very room. The place where each and every one of my *poems* have been transcribed. This book is not meant to be taken lightly but to be dug through and immersed within. If your mind begins to wander as you journey through my thoughts, take a moment, reflect, and then come back. I know that as a high school senior, that being open about emotions, and deep realities can seem too real for most. However, my hope for this book is not to profit from my writings, but rather for your own mind to take advantage of my sunderstanding about the reality of the world.

k.s

~~broken~~.

BREAKDOWN
   Br e a k down
      B r ea k do w n
         B r e a k dow n
            B   re   a k   d o w n
               broken.

            - k.s.

like broken glass,
i have been shattered
into millions of pieces.
broken.
left.
forgotten.
so please excuse my demeanor,
i can be a little
rough
around the edges.

- *forgotten sea glass*

we are all glass, when we shatter, we cannot heal,
but all the pieces are still there.

- you can be sea glass too

sticks and stones will break bones...
but words?
words will break hearts.

- *how am i still standing?*

i can see now
that you broke me,
just so you could
watch me
try and fail
to piece myself back together.

- how is the view?

lost

darkness rests in my heart,
and like an alley cat at night,
it cannot fully be seen without the possibility of pain.

- so, should i walk through?

i broke my back
carrying the weight of our relationship on my shoulders,
so i placed you down
so i could finally have some closure.

- *one sided*   *love*

lost

i struggled to reach the top of the water, waiting for a hand
to pull me up, but after a while of drowning, i stopped
moving, and finally felt the struggle disappear.

- professional swimmer

how is the view part two.

they say success is measured
by how much you change
the world,
yet
what if in reality, it is how much the world
changes you?

- *unsuccessful*

cracked?

you keep telling me your heart was broken by the past, yet i
see no crack, but after a while of getting to know you, i
realized I had put the pieces back. :)

- with love, your glue

many try to use their smile to change the world,
but end up having the world
change their smile.

- *still unsuccessful*

and she cried at the thought of death,
so i reminded her that she need not worry,
for in the end, we all become *lost* stories together.

- we write our own stories

f
  a
    l
    l
     i
      n
       g

off the cliff she leaped,
looking at the sky
she accepted this final relief.

the rush of wind
through her hair
–midflight a *wave* of regret
consuming every strand
–too late, next time, no point,
the light approaches,
no relief.

- another lost

why is it so
easy
to forgive others for what they did to us,
but so
hard
to forgive ourselves for letting them.

- am i forgivable?

you were the ache in my knees
that prevented me from standing

you were the knot in my
shoulders
that jolted me around

you were the limp in my leg
that kept me from moving on

and still you were also the crack
in my heart
that, piece by piece, finally made
me fall a p a r t...

- no longer standing

lost

in the ocean i begin to sink,
a wave consuming me,

flooding my thoughts,
flooding my mobility,

i cannot move,
i cannot stand up straight

what is happening to me?
i begin to sink lower against my will

however, i find that
instead of drowning in the ocean,
i was simply swimming deeper

- *why didn't i fight back?*

words

some mornings
i *ache* to feel
and although the timing isn't *ideal*,
it feeds my emotions
unable to give in,
i keep on suppressing
that ache that will never let me feel real.

- do you feel that?
please say it's not just me

bleeding through the pain
won't make it go away

but it will make it come to the surface
are you ready to face the red?

or are you trying to cover up scars
you aren't ready to share quite yet?

- *broken painter*

we rise, we fall,
we bury the dead, we become the buried,

we try, we fail,
we get back up,
and still they claim we are trying our best

we hope, we fear,
we love, we are hated,

we search, we lose ourselves,
but we cannot hide,
we cannot run,
for the thing we are running from
always ends up being the very thing

we chase.

- and i can't keep up

my own Hollywood set,
my very own chair,
i sit in waiting for the show to begin.

the director walks across the stage
the camera is rolling,
and the image of a child appears.

who is that?
a girl, so happy and so free,

who is that?
so small and so thin,

who is that?
with the sparkling eyes and the big grin

i ask,
who is that?

oh wait...
that little girl used to be me.

- *please don't make me watch the movie. please.*

Questionable Monster

For years scholars have questioned the true identity of a
monster.
From Frankenstein to his very own creation,
What does it truly mean to be monstrous?
Full of hate, lust, and desire?
Or are these *scholars* simply focused on traditional
appearance?
I would love to know whether they too believe,
The true monster begins with the one inside.

- i always thought you were the monster

and the soldier walked into war expecting a battlefield
but when she arrived all she saw was tears and sighs
she asked her friend,
"what is this, why do they cry?"
and all her friend could say back was,
"they are crying at the fact that they still are alive"

- the unexpected war within ourselves

love lost not gone.

she was so scared i would leave her, so she left me first.

- unexpected loss

love is never found where you expect it to be.
that's because love was expecting
you.

-the lost lover

and *finally*
the day came
where i could no longer ignore
the flame
in my brain
that lit my soul
on fire,
forever burning away the memories
you **ingrained** within me
until there was nothing left for me to remember.

- why won't you let me forget you?

lost

intermission: hey you

i hope by now you realize,
yes you,
reader of my thoughts,
reader of my misgivings
flashlight to my darkness,

i hope you realize because of the love,
the *love,* i have placed into your very hands,

that we are forever bonded
through words
through reactions
through tragedy.

- i hope you are still reading :)

the tragic part of endings is losing something that could
have been *everything*.

- so why does no one stay?

lost

as the soles of my shoes
help me to walk,
you are the blood
pumping through my veins to keep my heart from
stopping,
and the air through my lungs that allows me to keep
talking.

----

you are the roof of my house
that shelters me during a storm,
and the fountain of my life that keeps me longing for more.

- *addicted to love*

And just like that,
We were over as quickly as we began.

A flash,

A moment,

Now
just a memory.

- *love lost, not forgotten*

and when we finally meet,
i can tell you the memories i created
in my mind already

memories of
happy endings
that may never happen

memories of
words
that may remain unsaid

i can tell you my fears
i can tell you my hopes

and when we finally meet,
please...

please don't let me go

- *i cannot survive another love lost*

i loved you more than i loved myself.
you didn't break my heart...i did.

- *plot twist*

lost

if you stay,
and *if* we fall in love
together we would be stars in the sky,
                              bright,
                              beautiful,
yet gone before anyone can see us up close.

- the perfect constellation

don't
worry,
your
~~silence~~ hesitation
told
me
more
than
you
ever
could.

- the words unspoken

lost

if i grew a tree for every time i thought about you we could walk in my forest forever.

- *would you even walk through?*

know that you will be with me forever,
even when we grow old,
although i will lose you in my mind,
you will *never* be lost in my heart

- elderly love

The moon has phases and changes day to day,
But you and i?
We are forever whole.

- does this mean you complete me?

i loved you.
you hated me.
i lost you.
i found me.

- love isn't lost this time, just transferred.

lost

falling for something that isn't there
is *worse* than not falling
at all.

- i don't have a parachute...

will you catch me?

the saying goes,
"we were meant to meet, but not to be",

except we *were* meant to be,
you were just too *scared* to believe it.

- you shouldn't have left

Whole...

They say one day I will meet my other half.
That one day my other half will make me whole.

I always wondered why I felt so little,
I realize now it is because
I was taught that I am only half.

That I myself can *never* be fully happy alone.

- I AM NOT ~~WHOLE~~ HALF

Darling,
stop looking for love
around every corner
the day will come
when your heart
is ready
to handle
its weight.

~ not ready yet ~

i wish you could see:
your eyes when you gaze at a butterfly,
the bright grin as you walk in a field of flowers,
the fiery expression on your face
when you talk about your day,

but most of all,
i wish you could see how much love you deserve,
despite how little you long for compassion.

- *i can be your mirror*

you tell me it's hard to let go
of something
that's been there forever,

> but the truth is,
> it is even harder
> to move on,
> not knowing who you are
> without it.

- *nothing is forever*

be the person who tries
everything
just to make
somebody
feel

anything.

- *i'm here, i see you*

skipped

my heart   a beat when we met

but now my heart has stopped ticking,

my heart has stopped beating.

can you hear it?

because i think you have forgotten that

 i still have a heart...

- worn out clock *time's up*

she loved nature with all her heart
and wanted nothing more
than to be *just* like it.

so, she became beautiful,
or simply appeared so.

but she let people
use her,

and like the giving tree,
she gave in,

and stopped fighting.

- *thrown out flower*

Unknown

Her smile alone can light up a room,
Yet dig within her and there lies darkness too.
She wakes up, puts on her mask, one that conceals her fear
That nothing with last.

A girl with so many friends yet none,
A girl with a dream of finding the one.
Her mood changes with a flip of a coin,
And just like that she is full of joy.

With her long hair and her bright eyes,
She sees the world, yet hides what's inside.
If only this girl could let her pain seep through, maybe I
can show her I have darkness too.

- together we can smoke out the darkness

Her eyes were the gateway to her heart, her smile was a
shell for her pain, but her words?
her words made me breathless.

- *i can no longer breathe without her*

within each tear
there is a history of heart break.

each breathe she breathes
lies a sign at the end.

yet the tears she didn't shed,
still *stained* her cheeks.

but those around her
still turned their head.

- *escaped at last...*

galaxies form
stars collide
planets change
flowers bloom
rainbows appear,

yet
i just want to be here
laying with you.

- *you ~~are~~ were my world*

i once met a girl who longed to be with the stars.

her wish was granted when she decided she could fly.

imagination took over, and up up she went,
her bright eyes and big grin,
she leapt out into the sky,
and before she knew it,
all around her was black and white.

a secret world,
one unknown,
"if only they could see me now!"
she would groan,
climbing the white crystal stairs
wondering what lies within.

the sparkling castle appears before her eyes
a figure weighed over her like a tower,
but as the girl walked towards the mighty creature,
she stood *so* still.
for the girl realized,
this was not a new world,
she accomplished nothing,
in reality,
after her jump,

she fell.

- *angel, final loss.*

lost

hope?

earth,

if you could just rise above your clouds,
you might finally see our rainbow.

- with love the sky

lost

leave the world the same way you came
grateful for a chance at life,
yet ready for a whole new adventure

- *grown up baby*

words

obstacles are simply a neon arrow,
pointing us to the correct path.

- the road finally traveled.

To walk on a rainbow
Or up in the clouds,
On a path that leads me down,
I sit in waiting for the sun
To rise above my head
For tomorrow rushes in just as yesterday slowly fades
away.

- there is always hope in tomorrow

if every obstacle
is not an opportunity,
then why does every storm
create a new flower?

- water hope to keep it alive

lost

the girl only saw stars,
her sparkling eyes still shine,
because even through death she brings hope to the world
she captures the light in her supporters,

however,
as life went on
and as people left or died
that sparkle in eye decided to hide.
with no motivation darkness filled her being,
barrier broken,
she let evil spirits
emigrate
inside.
yet one day she met another girl,
just when she believed all hope was lost.
a tiny flitter of light began to emerge
locked eyes forged together like souls stuck in oblivion.

is it possible this girl has a little flame to spare?

- *if she does, would she even share?*

our power

does not come

in finding

the ways

we might

fall,

but seeing

the beauty

in the rise

- but what if i am paralyzed?

lost

and our eternal bond dissolved so quickly
as if it were eager to melt us all.
out of no where
hope was over.

- *no hope in this one*

imagine

imagine every dream was reality.
imagine every thought came to life.
imagine the success you hope for comes true.

our world lies within a galaxy,
lies within a universe,
lies within us.

And many say that we have,
"a world of possibilities, the world is our oyster",
and yet oblivion still remains out there,
a place where dreams can roam free.
but since imagination is deemed to be unlimited,
how come they keep setting our limit at the sky?

- demeaned dreamer

getting what you want,
is NOT always what you need.
embrace and love what is given,
for one day what you deemed an unexpected obstacle
might have been the lighthouse to your dreams.

- illuminated dreamer

footstep
    after
       footstep
          we continue to walk on.

hoping,
not to find a reason to live,
but to find the *person*
that gives us that reason.

- why can't i be that person?

hope is...

a random gesture that makes you smile,
a sunset that lures you into the night,
a glance that makes you want to stay for a little while,
and you know what? i think i just might.

hope is...

the glistening eyes of a baby as it stares in wonder.
the time a stranger helps you carry a heavy load,
or the lifeguard that keeps you from going under.

hope is...

the whistling of the trees,
the chirp of a bird that greets us in the morning,
the buzzing bees in the breeze
that might just make you freeze.

and yet...

                              most of us are still conforming.

- *blind to hope*

one word.
it only takes *one* word.
one word to prevent a tragic hero story,
one word to clear away the fog within a mind.
it only takes
one word.
you can prevent another loss

- you can be someone's hope.

even when your eyes are clouded by storms
even when the light can no longer overcome the dark
even when you feel like giving up,

the sun always rises,
the birds always chirp,
and the earth keeps turning,

you can keep rising with the sun,
you can keep talking to the birds,
and you *can* stop spinning in circles.

- *please, i can't lose another down the drain*

the perfect ending.

lost

the time approaches,
with every tik with every tok,
when the fatal choice emerges
and we must decide,
are we living
for the sake of being *alive,*
or are we only living in wait of death?

- too slow...
time's up

the saying,
"try to find the light in everyday"
is so important to remember because
if not,
you will never be able to go to the light in death

- *eternal darkness*

lost

anyone or any*thing*
that shows you
the value of living
is worth holding on to
until we must accept
fate.

- in death we part

if you are still reading...
my advice for you:
  - learn from your past
      - to experience the present
          - in longing for the future.

- k.s.

lost

no

one

ever

thinks

to

find

me

hiding

with

myself.

- trapped

timing doesn't have to be everything,
for we often plan for a tomorrow
that never arrives.

- *timeless*

lost

your pains seeps through you like a hungry tiger escaping
from a sheltered |prison|

- *who is the real animal?*

words

to mature is to adapt,
adjust to damage,
seeing who you can no longer trust.

being mature has *nothing* to do with age.

- damaged 17-year-old

Concern...

when you were mine,
you paid me no mind.

i called out for you
but you weren't there.

i asked for support
but received none.

you never checked up on me,
until the day they found me

dead.

that's when you showed your concern.

- *oh god, not another one-sided love*

within every blissful moment,
we fail to recognize its value
until it is only a memory

- *are we only a memory now? i haven't forgotten you.*

lost

is it possible that through death we are finally fully living?
i want to live fully.

- unalive

Goalkeeper

every sport has a goalkeeper.
someone whose job is to
prevent others from reaching their goal.
every life has a goalkeeper,
the person that never wants you to reach your goal,
out of fear that the chase will end,
and you will *finally*
                    move on.

- game over

lost

and just like that,
we were over as quickly as we began
a flash,
a moment,
now just a memory.

- *i cannot handle any more memories.*

the feeling arises,
the one in the pit of your stomach that aches.
the one that makes you feel like today is your expiration
date.
I certainly have that feeling,
but someone once told me,
"the ache isn't real",
that i just needed to rid my life
of heartbreaking surprises.

- do you ever feel that?

be not scared of oblivion
for your world ends every day,
but you always manage
to wake up in the morning.

~used to it~

people
>don't fear the dark,
>they fear what lies within.

people
>aren't afraid of heights,
>they afraid of falling.

and those
>who fear death,
>are actually afraid of not *living* while they are alive.

>- *what's* your *fear?*

You make me feel like I have lived a thousand lives in one
minute.
Every time we talk, my heart races towards the sun,
Simply your voice makes me smile,
Therefore, my blind eye hindered me from reality.
I became so entranced by the sound of your precious words
Every breath you breathed, a symphony.
But, after a while my eye began to heal,
And I realized how hideous your words truly were.

- *I'm still your mirror and I'm still blind*

All it takes is
One:
one **f**lutter—of a butterfly's wings
one **a**tom—inside a microscopic ant,
one **t**ear drop—that makes a splash turn into a wave,
one **e**pidemic—to cause
    To set in place.

- fate

the worst:

ever wondered what the three worst words are when put
together?
what monster created such a phrase
that could mean *so* much yet *so* little.
repeated infinity until death,
no longer when said is it being bold,
but it is also the worst lie i have *ever* been told.

- *"i love you"*

balloon

you came into my world light as a feather
i stared into your eyes and i knew,
one day you would fly,
fly as high as any balloon.
16 years of age, and you slowly sink down,
air spills out and my balloon can no longer turn around.
straight for the bottom,
deep down under,
the world will no longer see you glitter in the sky,
sparkle as you were, for you no longer wanted to fly.
grounded, i saw you staring back up to the top,
you were simply waiting for someone to love you...
but it is too late

pop.

- *i can't piece you back together, i'm sorry.*

lost

and when her eyes closed for the final time,
she took a deep breath,
and took off her virtual reality set.
"How was it?" God asked, "that was the only turn you get."

life is like a book,
we cannot skip chapters
because it is
hard. to. read.
we must *learn*
from those tragedies
in order for the

              perfect ending. 🔇

ABOUT THE AUTHOR

i didn't really know what to put here but this:
i am not a real writer.
this book is simply my thoughts put on paper.
my hope for this book
was not to worry,
was not to concern.
my hope for this book was to show what life is like for the
average 17 year old in 2020.
born in Manhattan, New York,
and later moved to Northern New Jersey,
i live a simple life and yet the challenges i face
are too complex for normal conversation.
i am just another teenager trying to survive.
:)

Made in the USA
Middletown, DE
08 October 2020